I0815323

SNAKES

MILK SNAKES

Cody Koala
An Imprint of Pop!
popbooksonline.com

Hello! My name is Cody Koala

This book is filled with videos, puzzles, games, and more! Scan the QR codes* while you read, or visit the website below to make this book pop.

popbooksonline.com/milk

*Scanning QR codes requires a web-enabled smart device with a QR code reader app and a camera.

abdobooks.com

Published by Pop!, a division of ABDO, PO Box 398166, Minneapolis, Minnesota 55439.

Printed in the United States of America, North Mankato, Minnesota.

042025
082025

THIS BOOK CONTAINS RECYCLED MATERIALS

Cover Photo: Shutterstock Images
Interior Photos: Alamy Stock Photo; Getty Images; Shutterstock Images
Editor: Elizabeth Andrews, Tyler Gieseke
Series Designer: Neil Klinepier, Colleen McLaren

Library of Congress Control Number: 2024948401

Publisher's Cataloging-in-Publication Data
Names: Murray, Julie, author.
Title: Milk Snakes / by Julie Murray
Description: Minneapolis, Minnesota : Pop!, 2026 | Series: Snakes | Includes online resources and index
Identifiers: ISBN 9781098247836 (lib. bdg.) | ISBN 9781098248376 (ebook)
Subjects: LCSH: Milk snake--Juvenile literature. | King snakes--Juvenile literature. | Milk snake--Behavior--Juvenile literature. | Snakes--Behavior--Juvenile literature. | Snakes--Juvenile literature.
Classification: DDC 597.96--dc23

Table of Contents

Chapter 1

Where Do They Live?

Milk snakes are a type of **king snake**. They live in many areas throughout North America and Central America. They also live in northern South America.

Watch a video here!

Where Milk Snakes Live

N
W
E
S

North America

Atlantic Ocean

Pacific Ocean

Central America

South America

Milk Snake Range

Milk snakes are found in forests, in open grasslands, and on rocky hills. They hide under rocks and in animal **dens**. They also live in barns and empty buildings.

Milk snakes can climb and swim but like to stay on land.

Milk snakes are often kept as pets. They are quiet and easy to care for. They can be handled through soft training. Milk snakes are not **venomous**.

The name *milk snake* comes from an old story that these snakes drank the milk of cows. Farmers found them in their barns. The snakes were there for the mice, not the cows!

Chapter 2

What Do They Look Like?

Milk snakes come in many different colors and patterns. Many are light brown with darker spots outlined in black. The spots can be red, dark brown, or black.

A milk snake has a light Y- or V-shaped mark on its head.

Learn more here!

Milk snakes have **mimic** features that keep **predators** away. Their colors make them look like **venomous** snakes such as the copperhead. Milk snakes also shake their tails to look like deadly rattlesnakes.

Milk snakes live for about 15 years in the wild.

A milk snake's body is covered in shiny **scales**. Most milk snakes grow to

Snakes shed their skin throughout their life.

be 2 to 4 feet (0.6–1.2m) long. Male milk snakes are bigger than females.

Chapter 3

How Do They Hunt?

Milk snakes are constrictors. They grab their **prey** with their teeth. Then, they wrap around it and squeeze. They eat their prey whole. Milk snakes eat mice, birds, frogs, and other snakes.

Explore links here!

Chapter 4

Baby Milk Snakes

Female milk snakes lay 6 to 24 eggs at a time. They lay them under rocks, in rotting logs, or in loose dirt. The eggs hatch about 50 days later. The babies are 6 to 10 inches (15–25cm) long.

Complete an activity here!

Making Connections

Text-to-Self

Would you want to see a milk snake in real life? Why or why not?

Text-to-Text

Have you read other books about snakes? If so, how were those snakes similar to or different from milk snakes?

Text-to-World

Milk snakes have patterns on their skin. What other animals have patterns on their skin?

Glossary

den – a safe resting place for wild animals, often underground.

king snake – any of a group of nonvenomous medium- to large-sized land snakes found from southeastern Canada to Ecuador.

mimic – to copy or imitate.

predator – an animal that hunts other animals for food.

prey – an animal that is hunted by other animals for food.

scales – small, hard, thin plates that cover reptiles.

venomous – producing a fluid, called venom, that is harmful to animals and humans.

Index

Online Resources

popbooksonline.com

Thanks for reading this Cody Koala book!

This book is filled with videos, puzzles, games, and more! Scan the QR codes* while you read, or visit the website below to make this book pop.

popbooksonline.com/milk

*Scanning QR codes requires a web-enabled smart device with a QR code reader app and a camera.